Registry of Guitar Tutors

LLCM & FLCM
Electric Guitar
Performance Diplomas
Handbook

**Compiled by
Tony Skinner and Merv Young
on behalf of
Registry Of Guitar Tutors
www.RGT.org**

Printed and bound in Great Britain

A CIP record for this publication is available from the British Library
ISBN: 978-1-905908-23-3

Published by Registry Publications

Registry Mews, Wilton Rd, Bexhill, Sussex, TN40 1HY

Cover photo by Michael Ruiz. Design by JAK Images.

Compiled by

The Specialists In Guitar Education
www.RGT.org

Contents

Page

4 ▶ CD Track Listing

5 ▶ Introduction

8 ▶ LLCM Technical Studies

18 ▶ LLCM Prepared Performance

20 ▶ LLCM Lead Improvisation

23 ▶ LLCM Rhythm Improvisation

28 ▶ LLCM Chart Reading

32 ▶ FLCM Performance

35 ▶ FLCM Programme Notes

36 ▶ Exam Entry

● CD track listing

1 ▸ **Tuning Guide**

2 ▸ **Technical Study No. 1**

3 ▸ **Technical Study No. 2**

4 ▸ **Technical Study No. 3**

5 ▸ **Lead Playing Sample Chord Progression No. 1**

6 ▸ **Lead Playing Sample Chord Progression No. 2**

7 ▸ **Lead Playing Sample Chord Progression No. 3**

8 ▸ **Improvised Rhythm Guitar Playing Example 1**

9 ▸ **Improvised Rhythm Guitar Playing Example 2**

10 ▸ **Chart Reading Example**

Introduction

This publication is the final volume in a progressive series of three Diploma handbooks aimed primarily at rock and pop guitarists who wish to obtain an accredited high-level performance qualification. Although the primary intention of these handbooks is to prepare candidates for the Registry Of Guitar Tutors (RGT) Performance Diplomas, the series provides a comprehensive structure that will develop the abilities of any guitarist – whether intending to take the diploma examinations or not.

Those preparing for an examination should use this handbook in conjunction with the *Syllabus for Diplomas in Electric Guitar Performance* and the *Electric Guitar Performance Diplomas Exam Information Booklet* – both freely downloadable from the RGT website: www.RGT.org

LLCM Outline

There are five parts to this Diploma examination, each of which is briefly outlined below:

❶ **Technical Studies.** This handbook contains the notation for three unaccompanied technical studies and the accompanying CD contains performances of them. The examination requires the candidates to select one of these to perform.

❷ **Prepared Performance.** The examination requires the candidate to perform an instrumental piece of their choosing.

❸ **Lead Improvisation.** The examination requires the candidate to perform a lead solo over a previously unseen chord progression. This handbook and the accompanying CD contain examples of the type of chord progression that will be presented.

❹ **Rhythm Improvisation.** The examination requires the candidate to improvise a rhythm part whilst following a previously unseen chord progression. This handbook and the accompanying CD contain examples of the type of chord progression that will be presented.

❺ **Chart Reading.** The examination requires the candidate to perform a previously unseen chart, which will contain some single-line notation and chords with a notated rhythm. This handbook and the accompanying CD contain examples of the type of chart that will be presented.

LLCM Marking Scheme

A maximum of 100 marks can be awarded during the LLCM exam. The maximum marks available in each section of the exam are shown below.

- Technical Study: 15
- Prepared Performance: 25
- Improvisation: 50   [Lead improvisation 25; Rhythm improvisation 25]
- Chart Reading: 10

Candidates who achieve a total of 75 marks or above will be approved to receive the LLCM Diploma certificate. Those whose mastery results in an award of 85 marks or more will receive the LLCM Diploma 'Upper Level' certificate.

FLCM Outline

There are two parts to this Diploma examination, each of which is briefly outlined below:

❶   **Prepared Performances.** The examination requires the candidate to perform a programme of music of their choosing lasting approximately 45 minutes. Pieces should mostly be performed either over backing tracks supplied by the candidate or with one or more accompanists supplied by the candidate, although up to 25% of the performance may consist of solo unaccompanied pieces if preferred.

❷   **Programme Notes.** The examination requires the candidate to supply original programme notes providing an in-depth harmonic and melodic analysis of the music performed.

Numerical marks are not awarded for FLCM Diplomas; each section will be marked as either 'Approved' or 'Not Approved'.

Entry Requirements

Candidates must normally have already passed the ALCM in Performance or Teaching electric guitar before entering for the LLCM examination, and LLCM in Performance or Teaching electric guitar before entering for the FLCM examination. However, candidates who feel they have relevant professional experience, and have attained the appropriate standard of performance, may apply to enter directly for either the LLCM or FLCM examination without holding previous qualifications. Such candidates would be expected to have secured local or regional recognition as a professional performer in order to gain direct entry to LLCM or to have secured national or international recognition as a professional performer to gain direct entry to FLCM. Such applications must be made in writing to the RGT Exams Office, accompanied by evidence such as press cuttings, reviews, CD recordings, etc., and supported by at least two references from professional musicians, who must not be the candidate's teacher.

Standard Required

The LLCM Diploma requires a professional standard of performance and musicianship; an extremely secure and versatile technique, together with convincing musicianship and interpretative skills, is expected.

The FLCM Diploma, the highest awarded by Thames Valley University, demands a truly exceptional demonstration of performing ability of the very highest standard. In order to pass, the candidate must present performances of a standard which one might expect to hear at a major concert venue, demonstrating a clear maturity of musical personality and interpretation.

It is highly unlikely that candidates without substantial playing and performance experience will possess the degree of technical ability and musical maturity required for success at these levels.

LLCM Technical Studies

Candidates should select and perform ONE of the three unaccompanied technical studies notated in this chapter.

The studies include techniques such as string bends, slurs, slides, harmonics, tapping, sweep-picking etc. Each of the studies is very different in terms of style and musical content, although each has been designed to equally assess a candidate's accuracy, fluency, coordination and control of the guitar.

Each study has been recorded on the accompanying CD to enable candidates to clearly hear how each one is expected to sound. Candidates are encouraged to listen to the tracks carefully to ensure that their performance is an accurate reproduction of the audio/notation.

Technical Study No. 1

This study features a combination of tapping, legato phrases and sweep-picking. The study has three distinct sections, with each section requiring a different set of playing techniques.

- The first section, from bars 1 to 6 inclusive, contains sextuplet legato phrases that are played using a combination of tapping, pull-offs and hammer-ons. The final note is played with vibrato using the fretting hand – not a 'whammy bar'.

- The second section, from bars 7 to 14 inclusive, starts with three one-bar phrases using double stops followed by descending legato lines. A linking bar of rapidly picked sextuplets leads to a development of the previous phrases incorporating a rhythmic variation of the double stops and a slide at the end of each of the three phrases. The double stop at the end of this section is played in natural harmonics by the fretting hand lightly touching the top two strings on fret 12.

- The third section, from bars 15 to 19 inclusive, contains a series of three ascending sextuplet legato phrases played using hammers-ons and pull-offs. After the first three phrases there is a short slurred run that descends the B string from fret 5. The three phrases are then repeated and followed by an ascending slurred run along the B string. The study finishes with an A minor arpeggio played with sweep-picking.

This study can be heard on CD track 2.

Technical Study No. 2

This expressive study contains three sections and focuses on a combination of string bends and legato techniques, as well as double notes and slides.

In order to encourage maximum individual expression, vibrato has been excluded from both the notation and the recording however, due to the style of this piece, candidates *are* expected to incorporate vibrato as an integral part of their performance of this study.

- The first section, from bar 1 to 10inclusive, features a series of phrases in A major played using string bends, pre-bends and legato techniques. Candidates should take care to ensure that the string bends, particular pre-bent notes, are pitched accurately.

- The second section, from bars 11 to 18 inclusive, is in the key of A minor and starts with a repeated series of arpeggiated notes with a descending bass line across six bars. Maintaining clarity, particularly of the open E string, is the main technical challenge here. This sequence finishes with an Eb diminished 7 chord in bar 17 and then an E major chord in bar 18 – the latter part of the bar played using artificial harmonics, by fretting the chord with the fret hand whilst touching the string 12 frets higher with a finger of the picking hand and simultaneously picking that string with another finger of the picking hand. Notice the *tenuto* lines over the first and last notes of most of the bars of this section indicating that these notes should be slightly emphasised, and the *rallentando* in bar 18 indicating a slowing of the tempo.

- The third section, from bars 19 to 23 inclusive, contains a series of descending, double note phrases in A minor that incorporate legato techniques and slides. This is followed by a bar containing a series of E major arpeggios ascending the fretboard and played *rallentando* before finishing with an E major chord; take note of the fermata sign on the final E note in bar 22. The study concludes with a slow Am(add4) arpeggio.

This study can be heard on CD track 3.

Technical Study No. 3

This lively study features legato techniques, chromaticism, octave shapes and fast picking.

- The first section, from bars 1 to 4 inclusive, contains two ascending chromatic-based sequences. The first two bars are played using hammer-ons; the next two bars are played by picking each individual note. This is followed by a 3 octave descending F# chromatic scale from bars 5 to 7. An ascending 3 octave G diminished arpeggio then takes over in bar 7 and continues into bar 8.

- In the next section, from bars 9 to the beginning of bar 14, there is a series of octave-based phrases. This commences with a descending, one octave Ab chromatic scale played in octaves. This is followed by the same scale ascending but with the octave split and the top note repeated three times.

- In bar 14 there is a descending Bb whole-tone scale that stops just short of three octaves. The study then concludes with the legato chromatic sequence that was featured at the very beginning.

This study can be heard on CD track 4.

Abbreviations used in the notation:

T	= tapping with a pick-hand finger
P	= pull-off
H	= hammer-on
S	= slide
Vib ⸯ	= vibrato
BU	= bend up (ascending string bend)
PB	= pre-bend (bend a string before picking it)
RP	= re-pick a string whilst the string is bent
BD	= bend down (allow a note to descend following a string bend)
L.V.	= let the notes ring
H12	= natural harmonic at the 12th fret
AH12	= artificial harmonic + fret number for the pick-hand finger to fret and simultaneously pick the string

Performance Tips

- You should perform your chosen study at approximately the stated tempo. Fluency and clarity are more important than speed for its own sake, and slightly slower or faster performances will be acceptable providing the tempo is maintained evenly throughout.

- There is no requirement to perform the study from memory, nor will any additional marks be awarded if you choose to play from memory.

- You should demonstrate accurate and fluent control over the instrument at all times, in an assured and confident performance.

- Distortion or other guitar effects can be used, *providing* all of the notes in the study can still be heard clearly. If you intend to use effects, you will need to bring your own effects units to the exam and set them up promptly and unaided.

- You are required to perform your selected study exactly as indicated in the notation and without any embellishment or variation of the rhythm or pitch.

- All the notes should be picked exactly according to the notation, i.e. played with the appropriate techniques such as hammer-ons, pull-offs, slides, etc. as indicated. However, as stated above, although vibrato signs have been deliberately omitted from Study 2, vibrato should be used to reflect the expressiveness of this musical style.

- You should ensure there is no lapse in the tempo when moving from one section or phrase to another. Each study should flow smoothly throughout.

- Ideally, you should follow the fingerboard positions indicated in the tablature for each study. However, alternative fingerboard positions will be acceptable provided the pitch, accuracy and musical content of the study is not compromised.

Technical Study No. 1

♩ = 92

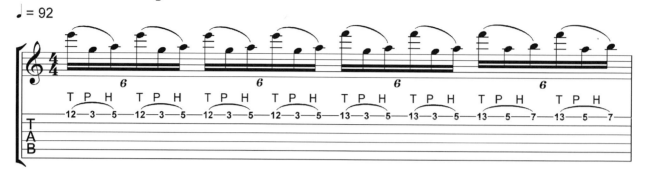

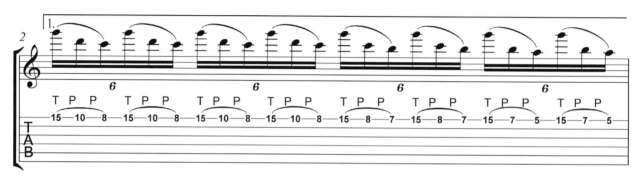

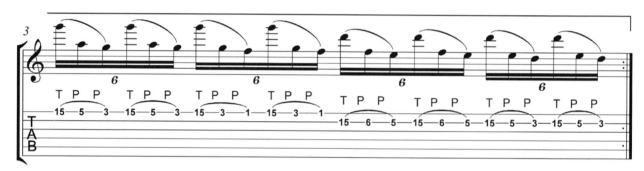

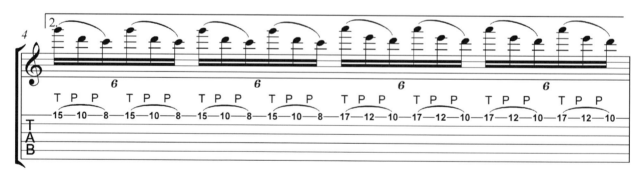

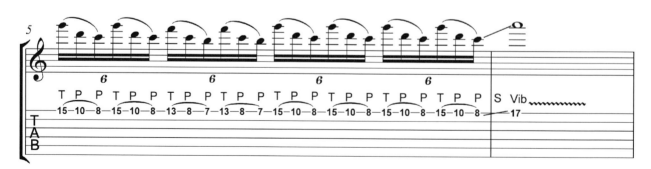

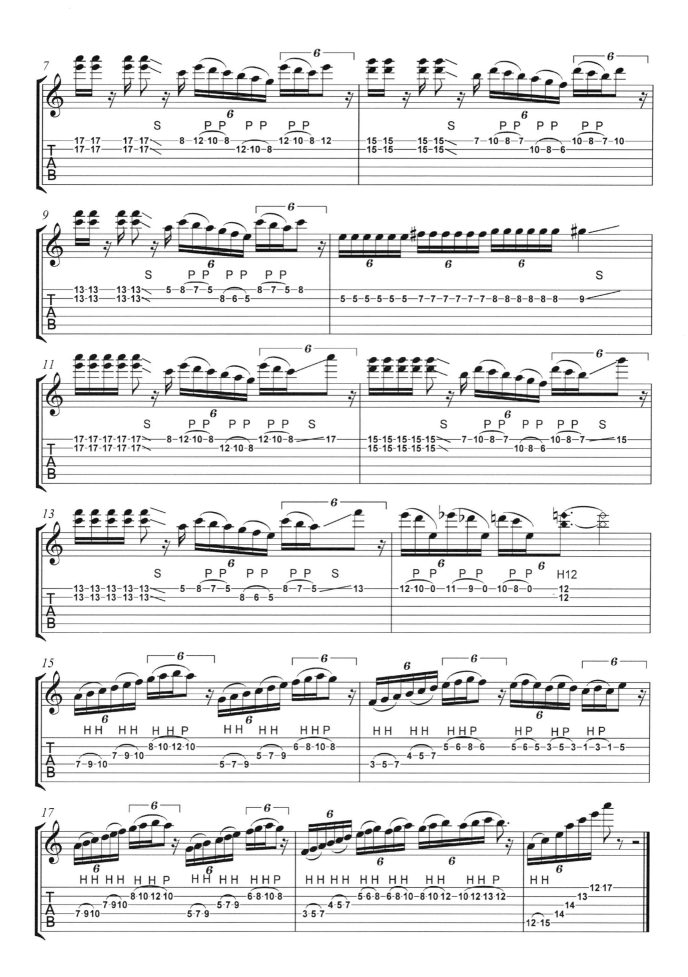

Technical Study No. 2

♩ = 72

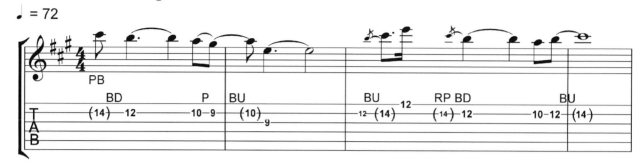

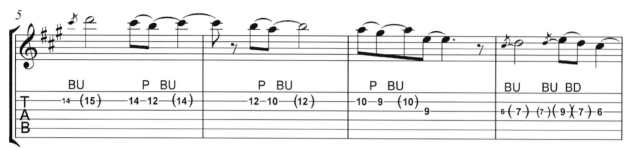

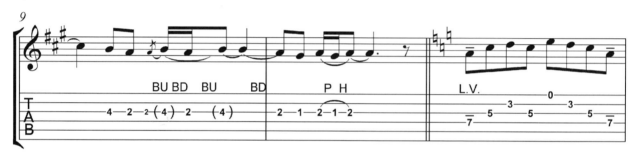

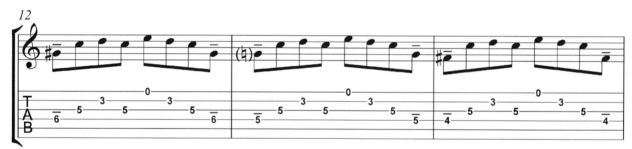

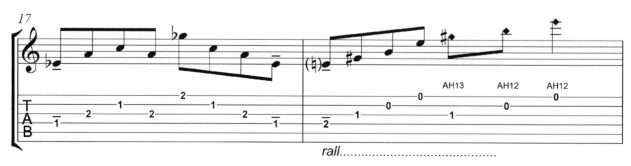

rall...

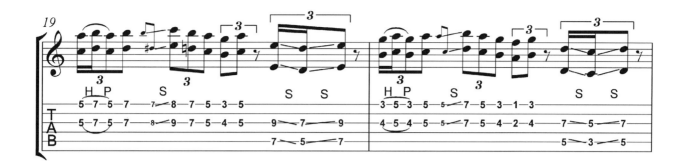

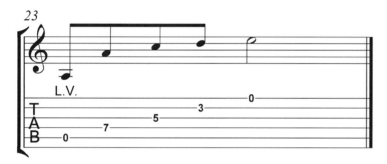

Technical Study No. 3

♩ = 132

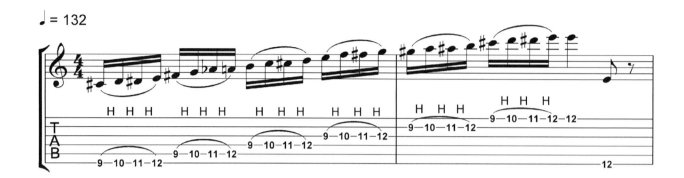

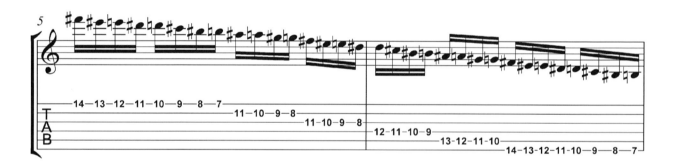

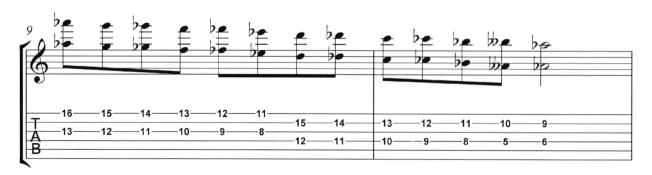

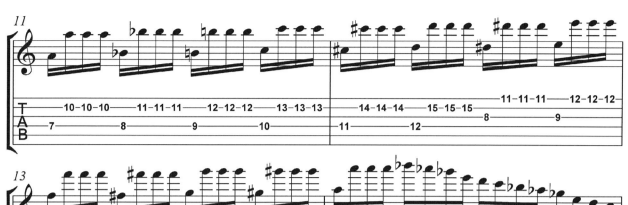

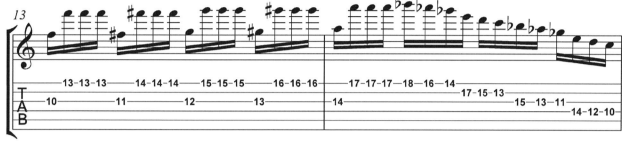

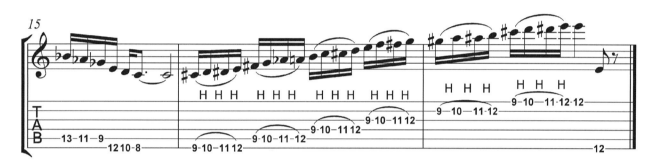

LLCM Prepared Performance

Candidates should select and perform *from memory* ONE instrumental piece using a backing track supplied by the candidate. The music can be a self-composition or an existing piece interpreted or arranged by the candidate. Marks will not be awarded for the composition itself, but for the demonstration of technical flair and creativity in performing the piece. The piece should last between three and six minutes. An electric guitar must be used for this section of the exam.

Although this is a 'free choice' section and candidates are expected to research appropriate music, the list of pieces below is provided to indicate the approximate standard expected at LLCM level. Further pieces may be listed on the RGT website (www.RGT.org) from time to time, however there is no obligation to choose any of these pieces; any alternative piece presenting a similar level of technical and musical challenge will be acceptable and candidates are positively encouraged to source alternative pieces to those listed here.

- **Cause We've Ended As Lovers (Jeff Beck)**

- **Sweet Dreams (Roy Buchanan)**

- **Room 335 (Larry Carlton)**

- **Revelation (Robben Ford)**

- **Orion (Metallica)**

- **Blues For Narada (Gary Moore)**

- **Tumeni Notes (Steve Morse)**

- **Nervous Breakdown (Brad Paisley)**

- **Always With Me Always With You (Joe Satriani)**

- **The Crusade (Trivium)**

- **The Animal (Steve Vai)**

- **Rude Mood (Stevie Ray Vaughan)**

- **Watermelon In Easter Hay (Frank Zappa)**

Whilst the list above contains only instrumental pieces, candidates are at liberty to select a piece to perform that originally contained a vocal melody line; in such an instance the vocal line should be reproduced and interpreted on the guitar as part of the candidate's arrangement – i.e. it should be performed in the exam as an instrumental (without singing).

Candidates may wish to select a piece to perform that in its original version is either less than three minutes in duration or longer than six minutes. In this instance the piece should be arranged so that the performance lasts for between three and six minutes.

Candidates may wish to interpret the main theme or melody of the piece they are performing by including their own melodic, harmonic and/or rhythmic variations compared to the original version. Whilst this is completely acceptable, candidates are advised to ensure that the original theme or melody is still clearly recognisable. Where the piece originally contains an improvised guitar solo, candidates can either reproduce this or alternatively can perform their own solo – providing this consists of a similar level of technical content as the original solo. Where the piece is a self-composition, candidates should ensure close reference to the supplied list of pieces to ensure the appropriate level of technical content.

<u>Standard Expected</u>

In order to obtain a high mark for this section, candidates should demonstrate a very high level of technical and musical accomplishment beyond that expected at ALCM level, as well as a consistently secure level of accuracy, fluency, clarity and articulation. The degree of musicality will be important and playing should demonstrate a mature sense of musical style. The performance should be confident and assured and should at all times communicate a clear sense of individual interpretative skill, with a clear ability to engage the listener fully in the performance.

Performance Tips

If your performance is of an existing piece of music you are encouraged to listen to the original artist's recordings of the track as well as sourcing live versions to gain further insight into the techniques and musical ideas used. If your performance is a self-composed piece you are encouraged to research a variety of existing music within similar musical genres to influence and inspire your playing.

At all times you are encouraged to be creative in your approach and express your individuality, whilst maintaining appropriateness to the musical genre.

Performances will probably be enhanced by incorporating, where musically appropriate, a variety of techniques such as slides, string bends, vibrato, slurs, tapping, sweep-picking, harmonics, double-stops, etc.

You can use either a clean or overdriven sound for this section of the exam. Any appropriate guitar effects can be used providing you can set them up promptly and unaided; the examiner is not permitted to assist with this and may ask you to proceed with the exam without the use of effect units if you are unable to set them up quickly and efficiently.

LLCM Lead Improvisation

Candidates will be presented with a previously unseen chord progression. Candidates are allowed one minute to study the progression and are then required to improvise a lead solo over the progression, which will be played by the examiner (either live or on CD).

After a one-bar count-in the chord progression will be played through five times without stopping. Candidates should not improvise during the first sequence of the chords, but rather listen and digest the tempo and style of the progression before improvising over the remaining four cycles. After the final sequence the progression will end on the first chord.

The chord progression will be in either $^4_4$ time or $^{12}_8$ time and will last for up to 16 bars.

The chord progression may be in any major, minor or blues-based key; although it will be predominantly diatonic there will be some non-diatonic chords and temporary changes of key. The examiner will not provide any advice or guidance regarding identifying the key or the scales or playing approaches to adopt.

Candidates should display a standard of improvisation beyond that expected at ALCM level, demonstrating secure and versatile technique and a clearly developed musical personality. Candidates should show a clear understanding of how to create an effective improvised solo that is accurate in terms of note selection, timing and phrasing in relation to the accompaniment.

Candidates are expected to demonstrate a confident display of variety in their choice of scales, arpeggios and playing techniques in a fluent and musically appropriate manner. In addition, candidates should be able to demonstrate an ability to make effective use of the full range of the fingerboard. This Diploma requires an effective performance that clearly demonstrates an assured sense of interpretative skill. Candidates should clearly demonstrate a perceptive and versatile approach to their choice and application of melodic and rhythmic ideas during their solo.

In addition, where musically appropriate, candidates are expected to be able to demonstrate a level of control over the application and execution of the following techniques that is worthy of a professional performance:

- String bending
- Vibrato
- Slurs
- Pick control

Example Chord Progressions

The following are examples of the type of chord progression candidates may be presented with in this section of the exam:

Lead Chart Example 1

○ CD track 5

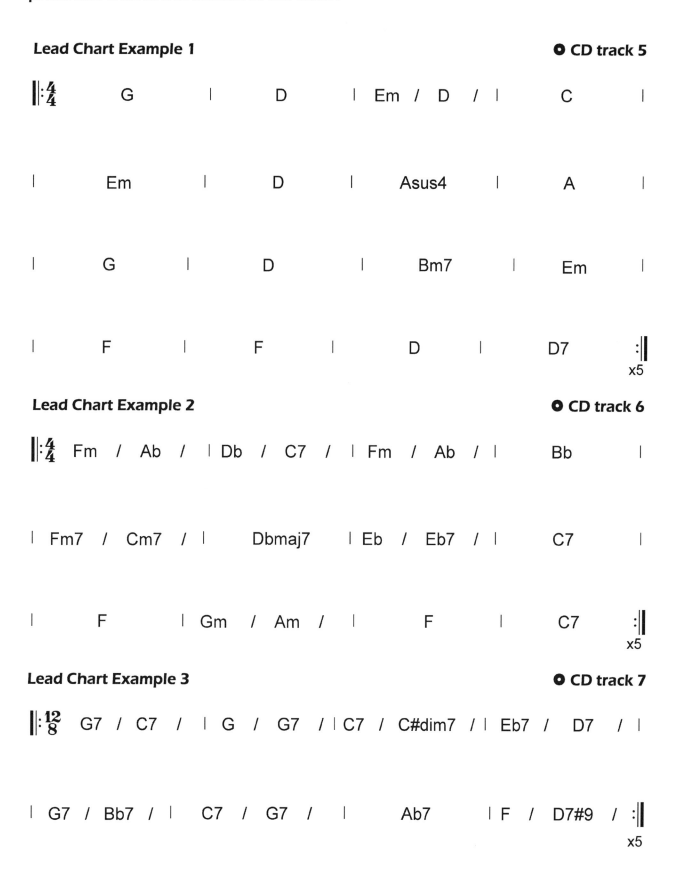

‖: 𝄴 G | D | Em / D / | C |

| Em | D | Asus4 | A |

| G | D | Bm7 | Em |

| F | F | D | D7 :‖
x5

Lead Chart Example 2

○ CD track 6

‖: 𝄴 Fm / Ab / | Db / C7 / | Fm / Ab / | Bb |

| Fm7 / Cm7 / | Dbmaj7 | Eb / Eb7 / | C7 |

| F | Gm / Am / | F | C7 :‖
x5

Lead Chart Example 3

○ CD track 7

‖: 12/8 G7 / C7 / | G / G7 / | C7 / C#dim7 / | Eb7 / D7 / |

| G7 / Bb7 / | C7 / G7 / | Ab7 | F / D7#9 / :‖
x5

21

It is important to note that the sample chord progressions provided in this chapter are supplied purely to provide examples of the *type* of chord progression that may occur in the exam. These examples are NOT the actual chord progressions that candidates will be given in the exam.

Performance Tips

For this section of the exam guitars should be tuned to Standard Concert Pitch (A=440Hz). The use of an electronic tuner or other tuning aid, prior to the exam or at the start of this section of the examination, is permitted.

Your improvised solo should be musically and stylistically appropriate to the style of the rhythm guitar accompaniment. While you are expected to demonstrate clear evidence of your own individuality, you should also be able to draw upon relevant musical influences to ensure a musically appropriate performance.

Performances may be enhanced by incorporating a variety of appropriate techniques such as slides, string bends, vibrato, slurs, double-stops etc. Where musically appropriate, you are expected to demonstrate fluency and confidence in the application of arpeggios and chromaticism. You are also welcome to use a range of other playing techniques, where musically appropriate, such as sweep-picking, finger-tapping, harmonics and whammy bar. This is your lead solo and your chance to demonstrate your own particular skills.

You are at liberty to use either a clean or distorted sound for this section of the exam. Similarly any other appropriate guitar effects can be used provided you can set them up promptly and unaided. The examiner will not assist with this and may ask you to proceed with the exam without the use of effects if you are unable to set them up very quickly and efficiently.

You will be presented with a chord chart that is typical of songs from a rock, pop or blues genre. You will notice from the examples given in this chapter that the chords and progressions have been deliberately kept relatively straightforward and, apart from the non-diatonic chords, are not overly complex in terms of harmonic structure or movement. This approach is designed to encourage you as the soloist to bring energy, interest and variety to the performance through your use of harmony, melody, rhythm and playing techniques.

You are expected to demonstrate versatility in your scale and arpeggio selection, although not at the expense of a fluent, melodic and confidently phrased performance. You should endeavour to demonstrate versatility, fluency and confidence in your approach to improvising your lead solo.

LLCM Rhythm Improvisation

Candidates will be presented with a previously unseen chord progression. Candidates are allowed one minute to study the progression and are then required to play the chords, improvising a rhythm part.

The chord progression will be in either $^4_4$ $^3_4$ or $^{12}_8$ time.

The range of chords presented will be restricted to the following:

- Major
- Minor
- Major, minor and dominant seventh
- Minor 7b5
- Diminished seventh
- Augmented fifth
- Sus 4
- Major and minor sixth
- Major, minor and dominant ninth
- 'Slash' chords (i.e. chords with non-root bass notes)
- Dominant seventh with either #5 or #9

The chord progression will be **predominantly** diatonic, although some non-diatonic chords may be included. The chord progression could be in any key.

Candidates should produce a standard of rhythm playing beyond that expected at ALCM level, demonstrating secure and versatile technique and a clearly developed musical personality. Candidates should display a clear understanding of how to create an effective improvised rhythm part that is accurate in terms of both chord selection and timing.

Candidates are expected to demonstrate a confident display of variety in their choice of chord shapes and playing techniques, and to incorporate these in a fluent and musically appropriate manner. This Diploma requires an effective performance that clearly demonstrates an assured sense of interpretative skill. Candidates should demonstrate clear evidence of a perceptive and versatile approach to their choice and application of rhythmic ideas during their performance.

Dynamic markings have deliberately not been included in the chord charts – in order to encourage candidates to use their creativity to create their own individual interpretation in this section of the exam; *the omission of dynamic markings does not in any way imply that dynamic variation should be absent from the performance.*

In order to obtain a high mark for this section, candidates should demonstrate a high level of technical accomplishment as well as a consistently secure level of accuracy, fluency and clarity, and a suitably varied dynamic range. The degree of musicality will be important and playing should demonstrate a mature sense of inventiveness and musical style.

Example Chord Progressions

The following are examples of the *type* of chord progression candidates may be presented with in this section of the exam. The first two examples have also been included on the accompanying CD – purely to provide examples of the approximate standard of playing and musicianship that is expected for a pass in this section of the exam; it is not intended to imply that candidates should replicate the musical ideas in the example tracks in their exam performance.

Slow blues O CD track 8

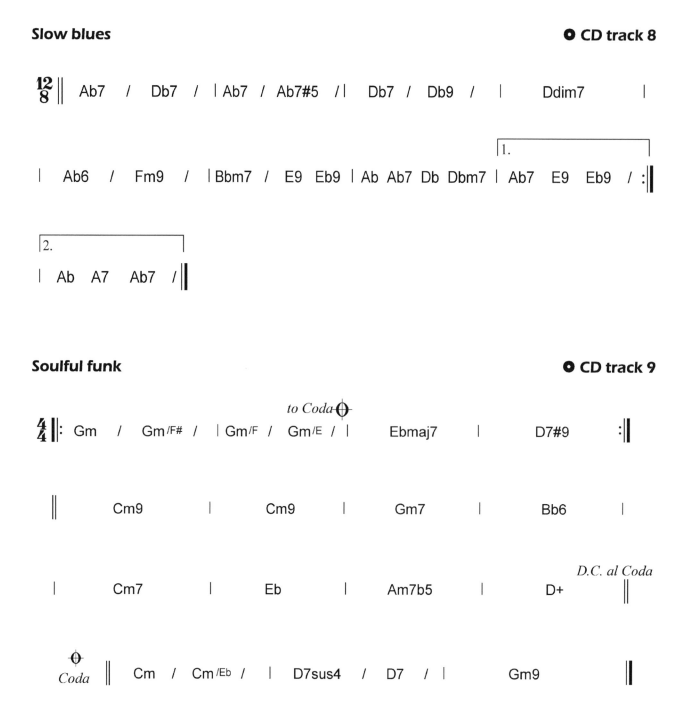

Soulful funk O CD track 9

Lively pop

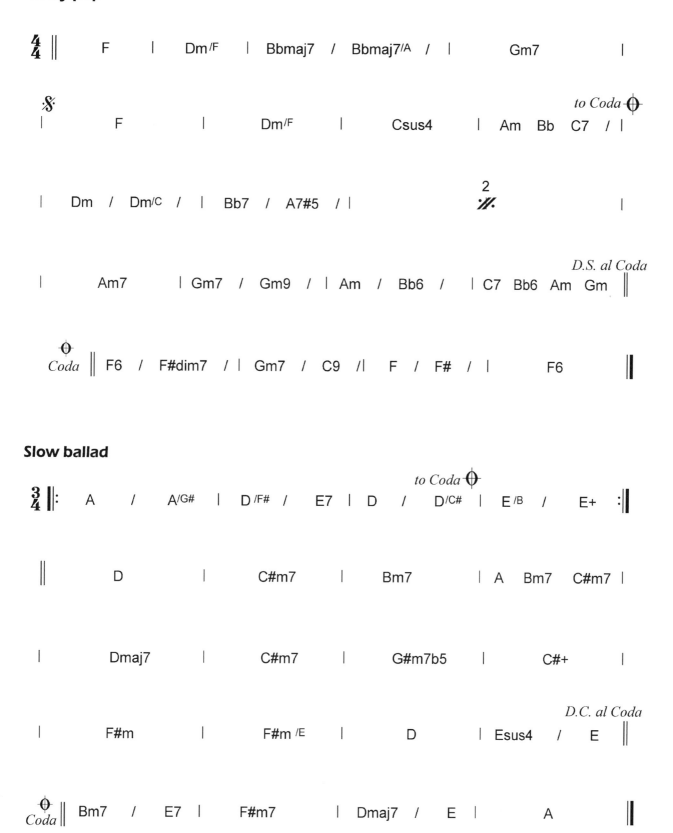

$\frac{4}{4}$ ‖   F | Dm /F | Bbmaj7   /   Bbmaj7/A   / | Gm7 |

𝄋 | F | Dm/F | Csus4 | Am   Bb   C7   / | *to Coda* ⊕

| Dm   /   Dm/C   / | Bb7   /   A7#5   / | 𝄎 2 |

D.S. al Coda

| Am7 | Gm7   /   Gm9   / | Am   /   Bb6   / | C7   Bb6   Am   Gm   ‖

⊕
Coda   ‖   F6   /   F#dim7   / | Gm7   /   C9   /| F   /   F#   / | F6   ‖

Slow ballad

to Coda ⊕

$\frac{3}{4}$ ‖:   A   /   A/G# | D /F#   /   E7 | D   /   D/C# | E /B   /   E+   :‖

‖   D | C#m7 | Bm7 | A   Bm7   C#m7 |

| Dmaj7 | C#m7 | G#m7b5 | C#+ |

D.C. al Coda

| F#m | F#m /E | D | Esus4   /   E   ‖

⊕
Coda ‖   Bm7   /   E7 | F#m7 | Dmaj7   /   E | A   ‖

Please note that the preceding chord progressions are supplied purely to provide examples of the *type* of chord progression that may occur in the exam. The above examples are NOT the actual chord progressions that candidates will be presented with in the exam.

During your performance you are expected to be able to interpret the following repeat signs that may be included on the chord chart:

Repeat dots:

Passages to be repeated are indicated by two vertical dots at the start and end of the section to be repeated. For example:

‖:   A | D   :‖   A | E   ‖

should be played as :

‖   A | D | A | D | A | E   ‖

D.C. (Da Capo – from the head) means play again from the beginning.
D.S. (Dal Segno – from the sign) means play from the sign (𝄋).

Al Coda (to the tail) means play the end section. This is marked with a coda sign (⊕).

'/.   Repeat the previous bar.

'//.   Repeat the previous bars (number above the symbol indicates the number of bars to repeat).

1st and 2nd time endings:

Bars marked ⌐1.   ⌐ are included in the first playing but omitted on the repeat

playing and replaced with the bars marked ⌐2.   ⌐
For example:

$\frac{4}{4}$ ‖:   A | A | D | E7   :‖   Bm | C#m   ‖

Should be played as:

‖   A | A | D | E7 | A | A | Bm | C#m   ‖

Performance Tips

Your rhythm performance should be musically and stylistically appropriate to the general style suggested by the title of the chord chart. Whilst you are expected to demonstrate clear evidence of your own individuality you should also be able to draw upon relevant musical influences to ensure a musically appropriate performance. The title of each chord chart also provides some general indication of the approximate tempo, but with the precise performance tempo being left to the discretion of the candidate.

As you are expected to demonstrate proficiency in a wide range of rhythm playing techniques, your performance will be enhanced by incorporating some of the techniques listed below, where musically appropriate.

- Different fingerboard positions of the same chord: a variety of chord voicings, including the use of open chords, barre chords and partial chords.
- Use of extended or altered chords to embellish the basic chord symbols.
- A range of strumming styles.
- Plectrum and/or fingerpicking arpeggiation.
- Single or double-note licks between chords.
- Splitting chords between bass and treble parts.
- String-damping (both fretting-hand and strumming-hand).

You are required to use a clean rather than distorted sound for this section of the exam. However, any other appropriate guitar effects can be used provided you can set them up promptly and unaided. The examiner will not assist with this and may ask you to proceed with the exam without the use of effects if you are unable to set them up very quickly and efficiently.

LLCM Chart Reading

Candidates will be presented with a previously unseen chart in $^4_4$ time that will include chord symbols with a notated rhythm part, as well as some single-line melodic parts in standard notation. Candidates are allowed five minutes to study the chart and are then required to play it, following the notated rhythm and melody notation.

The range of chords presented will be restricted to:
- major;
- minor;
- major 6;
- major 7;
- minor 7;
- dominant 7;
- dominant 9;
- dominant 7 #9;
- minor 7b5;
- sus 4;
- power (5th) chords.

The chart will be *predominantly* diatonic, although some non-diatonic chords and melody notes may be included. The key range will be limited to those keys generally used in pop and rock music. Some common repeat signs may be included.

In order to obtain a high mark for this section, candidates should demonstrate a consistently secure level of accuracy, fluency, clarity and articulation, in a confident and musical performance featuring effective use of dynamics.

Candidates are at liberty to use either a clean or distorted sound for this section of the exam, provided the overall musical result can be heard clearly.

Example Charts

On the following pages are examples of the *type* of chart candidates may be presented with in this section of the exam. The first example has also been included on the accompanying CD – purely to provide an example of the approximate standard of playing and musicianship that is expected for a pass in this section of the exam.

Moderate tempo

Fairly fast

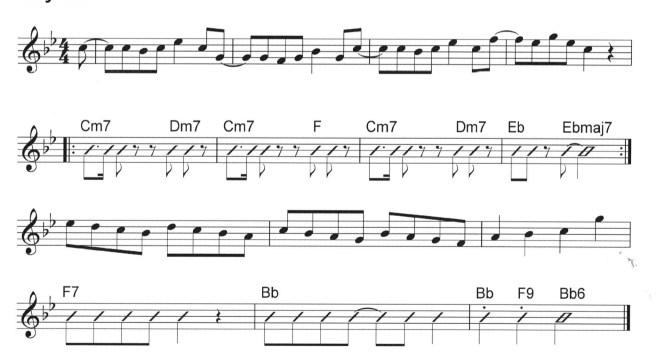

Moderate tempo

Lively

Please note that the preceding charts are supplied purely to provide examples of the *type* of chart that may occur in the exam. The above examples are NOT the actual charts that candidates will be presented with in the exam.

Performance Tips

- Each chart includes a broad indication of tempo, however accuracy, fluency and clarity are more important than speed for its own sake, providing the performance tempo is not unduly laboured.

- You should demonstrate accurate and fluent control over the instrument at all times, in an assured and confident performance.

- You are required to perform the chart exactly as indicated in the notation and without any embellishment or variation of the rhythm, melody or harmony.

- In order to encourage candidates to display their creativity, dynamic markings have not been included in the chord charts; *the omission of dynamic markings does not imply that dynamic variation should be absent from the performance* – you should incorporate musically appropriate dynamic variations into your performance.

FLCM Performance

Candidates should compile and perform a varied programme of music of approximately 45 minutes duration. All pieces must be performed *from memory*. The programme can consist of self-composed or existing pieces arranged and interpreted by the candidate. Although candidates are encouraged to use their own compositions within the programme, marks will not be awarded for the composition itself, but for the demonstration of technical flair and creativity in performing the pieces. The pieces should mostly be performed either over backing tracks supplied by the candidate or with one or more accompanists supplied by the candidate.

If preferred, up to 25% of the total performance time may consist of solo unaccompanied pieces. But do note that as this is a specialist electric guitar performance Diploma, an electric guitar must be used throughout this exam.

Although this Diploma allows a 'free choice' of music to perform, candidates are expected to research appropriate music that will demonstrate their electric guitar playing skills and the range and breadth of their musicianship to the maximum. The list of pieces below is provided to indicate the approximate standard expected at FLCM level. Further pieces may be listed from time to time on the RGT website (www.RGT.org), however there is no obligation to choose any of these pieces; any alternative piece presenting a similar level of technical and musical challenge will be acceptable and candidates are positively encouraged to source alternative pieces to those listed here.

- It Was Only Yesterday (Larry Carlton)

- Erotomania (Dream Theater)

- Eudaimonia Overture (Paul Gilbert)

- Cliffs Of Dover (Eric Johnson)

- Get You Back (Shawn Lane)

- Blitzkrieg (Yngwie Malmsteen)

- Hot Wired (Brent Mason)

- Flying In A Blue Dream (Joe Satriani)

- Die To Live (Steve Vai)

- Lenny (Stevie Ray Vaughan)

When compiling their programme of pieces to perform for this Diploma, candidates should bear in mind the need to display a broad stylistic awareness and ability in performing more than one narrow genre of music. Whilst some degree of stylistic specialisation is acceptable, candidates should endeavour to include some variety of style, mood and tempo within their programme as a means of actively displaying the full range and breadth of their musicianship and playing ability.

Although the previous list contains only instrumental pieces, the performance may include vocals – either by the candidate or a separate vocalist. In this case candidates must ensure that the guitar parts are prominent and sufficient enough to fully display the candidate's guitar playing skills. Candidates are also at liberty to select a piece to perform that originally contained a vocal melody line and perform this as an instrumental. In such an instance the vocal line should be reproduced and interpreted on the guitar as part of the candidate's arrangement – i.e. it should be performed in the exam as an instrumental (without singing).

Candidates may wish to interpret the main theme or melody of the piece they are performing by including their own rhythmic, harmonic and/or melodic variations compared to the original version. Whilst this is completely acceptable, candidates are advised to ensure that the original theme or melody is still clearly recognisable.

Where the piece originally contains an improvised guitar solo, candidates can either reproduce this or alternatively can perform their own solo – providing this consists of a similar level of technical content as the original solo.

Where the piece is a self-composition, candidates should ensure close reference to the supplied list of pieces to ensure the appropriate level of technical content.

Standard Expected

Candidates should bear in mind that FLCM is the highest Diploma of London College of Music, and is considered as an equivalent qualification level to a Master's Degree. In order to obtain a high mark for this section, candidates should demonstrate a level of technical and musical accomplishment of the highest professional standard.

It is the responsibility of the candidate to ensure that any 'own choice' pieces are of a technical standard appropriate to this Diploma. The candidate's list of selected repertoire may not be submitted in advance for approval, as the standard of *performance* of any pieces can only be reliably assessed by examiners during the actual examination. Where the selected repertoire does not enable the candidate to demonstrate mastery at this level, the examination assessment will reflect this. Therefore, candidates should select their pieces with care, in order to provide an interesting, balanced and varied programme that demonstrates a wide range of technical and expressive contrasts.

The performance should be worthy of a prestigious music venue, and should include a consistently secure level of accuracy, fluency, clarity and articulation. The degree of musicality will be important and playing should demonstrate a fully mature sense of musical style. The performance should be confident and assured and should at all times communicate a clear sense of individual interpretative skill, with a clear ability to engage the listener fully in the performance.

Performance Tips

If your performance is of an existing piece of music you are encouraged to listen to the original artist's recordings of the track as well as sourcing live versions to gain further insight into the techniques and musical ideas used. If your performance is a self-composed piece you are encouraged to research a variety of existing music within similar musical genres to influence and inspire your playing.

At all times you are encouraged to be creative in your approach and express your individuality, whilst maintaining appropriateness to the musical genre.

Include some variety of style, mood and tempo in your programme so that you give yourself the optimum opportunity to display the full extent of your musical range and playing abilities.

Performances will probably be enhanced by incorporating, where musically appropriate, a variety of appropriate techniques such as slides, string bends, vibrato, slurs, tapping, sweep-picking, harmonics, double-stops etc.

You can use either a clean or overdriven sound for this section of the exam. Any appropriate guitar effects can be used providing you can set them up promptly and unaided; the examiner is not permitted to assist with this and may ask you to proceed with the exam without the use of effect units if you are unable to set them up quickly and efficiently. Any accompanists involved in the performance need to supply and set-up their own equipment.

The FLCM performance may take place in front of an audience, such as at a concert, provided that this has been agreed in advance with the RGT Examinations Office and that it this does not affect the normal examination procedure (e.g. intervals are not permitted). You should make all efforts to demonstrate an awareness of stagecraft appropriate to the style of music being performed.

FLCM Programme Notes

Candidates should prepare and supply original programme notes providing an in-depth harmonic and melodic analysis of the music performed. These programme notes must be typewritten and should in total be between 1000 and 1500 words. Two copies of the programme notes should be taken to the examination and handed to the examiners.

You should incorporate the following information in the programme notes:

- Titles and composers of the pieces performed as well as details of the original artist/s where the pieces are not self-composed.

- A brief outline of the reasons behind your choices, in particular outlining how you feel these pieces influenced the structure and flow of the performance as a whole.

- An analysis of any prominent harmonic, melodic and rhythmic features of the pieces performed. This should include an identification of the keys used and any modulations, the time signatures and any variations within each piece as well as highlighting any changes in tempo. The harmonic structure should also be explored providing detail on the chord structures as well as the use of any harmonic devices such as pedal notes, circle of fifths, chord embellishments etc. The approaches to any improvised sections should also be outlined with information on the scales adopted, any use of arpeggios or chromaticism, use of melodic devices such as repeated rhythmic motifs or question and answer phrasing. You should also consider the impact each of these prominent features had on the pieces and the performance as a whole.

- An analysis of the dynamic content of the pieces and the performance as a whole. This should include an identification of any prominent changes in volume and tempo and the reasons for their inclusion.

- For any pieces that were originally performed by another artist you should identify any areas where your rendition differs significantly from the original version. For pieces that are self-composed, or have not been previously recorded, you should explain how the music developed into the piece you performed.

- An outline of the techniques employed in each of the pieces. For instance, the use of sweep-picking, two-handed tapping, hybrid-picking and so on. In each case candidates should state the reasons for using these techniques, highlighting what they brought to the music.

- An overview of any guitar effects that were used during the performance stating the reasons behind the equipment that was used and how this affected the pieces that were performed.

Exam Entry

An exam entry form for both LLCM and FLCM can be downloaded from the RGT website [www.RGT.org], where a current entry fee list can also be viewed. Candidates without internet access should send a large stamped self-addressed envelope, with a short letter requesting a Performance Diploma entry form and fee list, to the RGT office [RGT, Registry Mews, 11-13 Wilton Rd, Bexhill, TN40 1HY]. Non-UK candidates should contact their RGT national representative for information on entry procedures.

Do remember that candidates must normally have already passed the ALCM in Performance or Teaching electric guitar before entering for the LLCM exam, and LLCM in Performance or Teaching electric guitar before entering for the FLCM exam, although candidates with relevant professional experience may apply to enter for either exam without holding previous qualifications – see page 6 of this handbook for further details.

More Information

Candidates should read the Electric Guitar Performance Diploma Exam Syllabus and Exam Information Booklet prior to entering the exam. These can be downloaded from the RGT website: www.RGT.org
Candidates without internet access should send a large stamped self-addressed envelope to the RGT office: RGT, Registry Mews, 11-13 Wilton Rd, Bexhill, TN40 1HY.

Other RGT Examinations

In addition to the Performance Diplomas covered in this handbook, RGT also offers the less advanced diplomas of ALCM (Associate Diploma of the London College of Music) and DipLCM (Diploma of the London College of Music).

RGT also offers a full range of professional guitar teaching diplomas: DipLCM(TD), ALCM(TD) and LLCM(TD). A comprehensive range of pre-diploma graded exams for electric, acoustic, bass and classical guitar is also available, as well as graded exams in popular music theory.

Exam Information Booklets for all these exams can be downloaded from the RGT website: www.RGT.org